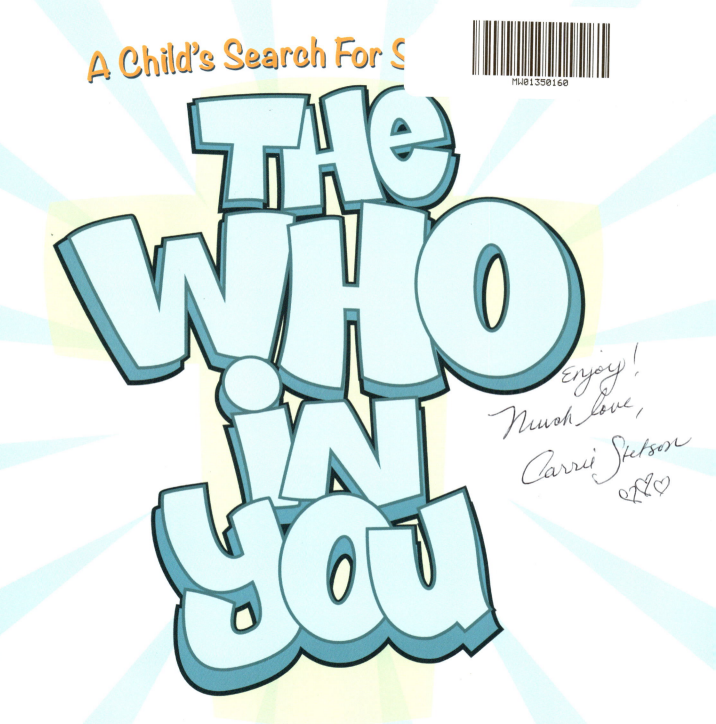

For further information please visit the website at www.whoinyou.com
© 2013 by Carrie Stetson
All rights reserved. No part of this publication may be reproduced, stored in a retrieval system, or transmitted in any form or by any means--for example, electronic, photocopy, recording--without prior written permission of the author. The only exception is brief quotations in the printed reviews.

Written by Carrie Stetson
Illustrated by Heather Branscom
Design & Layout by Jim Deasy

Published by Christian Equippers International
3580 Blackwood Road
South Lake Tahoe, California 96150
www.equipper.com

ISBN-10: 098974910X
ISBN-13: 978-0-9897491-0-7

When I first read this book I was brought to the consideration of how wonderful but vulnerable childhood is. My own memories went back to times of my mother praying simple prayers over me as she tucked me in and drifting off to sleep in the security of her love. But I also remembered the fears and insecurity facing situations when she wasn't there—the first day of school, times of being bullied, and concerns about where I fit in. Jesus said, "let the little children come to me" (Matt. 19:14). This little book does just that. I picture parents reading it not just once, but many times to their children and the Holy Spirit working within the listening child to bring him or her to the "Who" in them that makes their life safe and their identity meaningful and secure, the One who is always there and who always cares!

Terry Edwards
Pastor/Lake Tahoe Christian Fellowship

This book belongs to:
_____

This book is dedicated to my adorable grandson Luke.
As you accomplish great things in life, may you always find your significance in being cherished and loved by **"The Who in You"**.
Hugs and Kisses,
Grandma Carrie

The Who in You

Did you know that you have a best friend that you can't even see?
So where do you look to find this wonderful, invisible friend?
I'll give you a clue.... He's closer than you think!

Follow Luke's exciting journey to discover the "**Who**" in him!

I'm looking for the Who in me–

    The one who I am meant to be.

I'm looking for the best in me!

Looking...

       Looking...

              Looking...

How do I find the Who in me?

I'm looking to find
the Who in me,

The one I am
when I feel free!

He draws me in,
    to cuddle in His arms,

I feel so safe and special,
    I know I won't be harmed.

Yes, I know I'm forgiven,

I forgive others too,

I feel so free and happy,

and all over new!

Jesus smiles, and I smile back, He whispers this to me:
 Listen, and I'll tell you about the Who in you - It's ME!
  I made you to be free. I made you to be YOU...with ME!

I LOVE YOU...
Whether you are short or tall, big or small
Big feet, little feet, smelly feet and all!

Wherever you are, Whatever you do, I am always smiling at you.
LOVE is always smiling at you!

You don't have to go looking near or far...
I'm always with you, wherever you are.

I made your heart, I made your ears, I made your eyes,
I made your mouth. I made your kind heart to love Me,
Your smart ears to hear Me, Your bright eyes to see Me,
Your smiling mouth to sing with Me,
And talk with Me...

Now I know the WHO in me—
It's Jesus Christ who makes me free!

Let's Talk!
Parent-Child Communication Tool

This story of Luke's journey and discovery offers a great opportunity to have a conversation with your child regarding issues of their own identity and sense of significance. Following are some optional approaches you may choose that would help them open up to you and receive prayer for some important issues:

1. Ask your child if they understood what the boy in the story was looking for and what he discovered. Ask your child if they have ever felt like this boy. Ask if they understand how Jesus could be the answer to this boy's search. Explain as is necessary.

2. Explain to your child that as we grow up we sometimes have questions about ourselves such as, "Why am I here?"...or "Does God really like me?"...or "Am I a good kid?" Ask if they ever have questions like this? (Pause and let your child answer) Respond to your child by addressing their concern and telling him or her how special and valuable they are to both God and yourself.

3. Describe how Luke discovered who He was in the eyes of God and how it made him feel so good about himself and free inside. Ask your child if they feel God's love and care for them. If not, ask if they have received Jesus as their Saviour and if they have not, ask them if you can pray with them to do so. Have them repeat after you. If they have already received Jesus Christ, ask if you can pray for them to feel closer to Him. Pray a blessing over them to feel His love and nearness and that their hearts would be filled with love for God.

4. (Parent to child) Ask your child if there is anything in their life right now that they would like you to pray for them—any fear or problem that may be affecting them. After you pray, ask them if they feel better now.

Finish your time together by telling your child how much you love them and give them a kiss or hug.

Author Carrie Stetson is an RN, Certified Health and Wellness Coach and Speaker. She is passionate about people becoming healthy and whole in their body, soul and spirit.

Along with her husband Steve, she is part of the pastoral team at Lake Tahoe Christian Fellowship in Lake Tahoe, California where she is also the director of an inner healing ministry, Bethel Sozo.

Besides Steve, her other great treasures include her two beautiful daughters, Melissa and Natalie, and of course her impossible-not-to-love grandson, Luke!

Helping people walk through the process of freedom and wholeness into their destiny is a great joy for her. Carrie is thrilled when young and old alike discover and celebrate how incredibly valuable and loved they are!

www.whoinyou.com

Heather Branscom | Illustration
www.heatherbranscom.com

Jim Deasy | Design & Layout
www.jimdeasy.com

In Honor of Susie.

CPSIA information can be obtained at www.ICGtesting.com
Printed in the USA
LVIW01n0200101015
457722LV00002B/2